Leaving
A
Godly Legacy

David P. Therrien

DEDICATION

Dedicated to Paul (Pauley) Andrade Jr. who has certainly left a legacy of love and Godliness.

CONTENTS

INTRODUCTION

Life is a gift and it takes great wisdom to live a life of significance. Many aspects of who we are and what we do go into what makes up our lives. One of the more important issues of life has to do with remembrance. How often do we consider how people will remember us? This books is about the value of leaving a sweet memory in the minds of people who knew us and watched us as we journeyed through life.

Your reputation is how you are remembered while you are alive. Your legacy is how you are remembered after you are gone. Hopefully, this is important to you and may this book help you to leave a Godly legacy.

CHAPTER 1
JESUS LEFT A LEGACY

"Legacy" is from the Latin word "to bequeath" or anything handed down as from an ancestor. In "Leaving A Legacy"` we are going to examine several things that you can "hand down" to the following generation for their blessing. And you're going to be surprised how easy it can be.

People are sometimes remembered by what is placed on their tombstone. If people were to remember you, what do you think they would read on your tombstone? This is something we want to consider while we are alive.

Jesus handed down two legacies through which He is remembered. He left us the Lord's Supper and the Great Commission.

The Lord's Supper is also called the Lord's Table, or Communion and it is an observance, acceptance and remembrance of what Jesus did for us in sacrificing Himself for the sins of the world. Jesus handed it down to His disciples and then, personally revealed it to the Apostle Paul through the Holy Spirit. Let's go back to that upper room and look in on the last meal Jesus had with His disciples.

They were eating the Passover meal and Judas had left to betray the Lord. We find the account in Matthew 26:26-28.

While they were eating, Jesus took some bread, and after a blessing, He broke it and gave it to the disciples, and said, "Take, eat; this is My body."

And when He had taken a cup and given thanks, He gave it to them, saying, "Drink from it, all of you; for this is My blood of the covenant, which is poured out for many for forgiveness of sins.

This legacy is called a "sacrament." A sacrament is a ritual, something ceremonial or symbolic. Mark and Luke, two other disciples also recorded this event.

The Apostle Paul was not present at the upper room Passover meal. He was actually a persecutor of the church after Jesus left these sacraments. He finally met the Lord on the road to Damascus and had a spiritual awakening. He realized that by persecuting Christians, he was persecuting Christ. But in his first letter to Corinth he speaks of how God gave him a revelation about the Lords' Supper and its significance.

For I received from the Lord that which I also delivered to you, that the Lord Jesus in the night in which He was betrayed took bread... I Corinthians 11:23

The Upper Room Scene

While they were eating, Jesus took some bread,

and after a blessing, He broke it and gave it to the disciples, and said, "Take, eat; this is My body."

The bead represented the pure and sinless life that Jesus led. His innocent life qualified Him to be the Savior of the world.

"And when He had taken a cup and given thanks, He gave it to them, saying, "Drink from it, all of you; for this is My blood of the covenant, which is poured out for many for forgiveness of sins."

Jesus had "given thanks" for the cup which represented His shed blood for the sins of the world. He was actually thankful that He could sacrifice Himself for us. He stated that He was establishing a new covenant. A covenant is a contract between two parties by which they are mutually bound to do certain things. This covenant was often ratified by the slaying of a sacrificial animal and its blood poured out. The new covenant replaced the Mosaic Law and ushered in the age of Grace. We now have the privilege to enter into the presence of God on our own without a representative.

Hebrews 10:19 tells us, "Therefore, brethren, since we have confidence to enter the holy place by the blood of Jesus."

This covenant was between the Son and the Father. It was their agreement that Jesus would die for the sins of the world and the Father would save all those who believe in the Son and the sacrificial work He did on the cross.

Jesus left us the legacy of the communion table so we would remember the offering of Himself for our sins and for the sins of the world. This is how He wants to be remembered.

The next and last legacy Jesus left us is known as The Great Commission found in Matthew 28:18-20.

And Jesus came up and spoke to them, saying, "All authority has been given to Me in heaven and on earth. Go therefore and make disciples of all the nations, baptizing them in the name of the Father and the Son and the Holy Spirit, teaching them to observe all that I commanded you; and lo, I am with you always, even to the end of the age."

This legacy was to remind His followers to make disciples of all nations, to help them to become followers of Christ and to baptize them in water, demonstrating their identity them with Him. This legacy from Jesus has been passed down to every generation for 2,000 years. It is the basis for the work of the church and the growth of the Kingdom. When you understand the importance of the legacy that Jesus left, this may help you to see that your legacy is important as well.

CHAPTER 2
HOW TO LEAVE A GODLY LEGACY

Our lives consist of several facets. They are relational which concerns our family and friends; vocational which concerns our quality of work and recreational which is how we spend our free time. What we do with these facets of our life will determine how we will be remembered long after we are gone. We will all leave some type of legacy. Our legacy will concern those three facets of life; how I a remembered by the work that I did, by my family and friends and how I expressed myself through hobbies. It may be positive or it may be negative, but we will leave a legacy. Adolph Hitler left a negative legacy. Abraham Lincoln left a positive legacy. Judas Iscariot left negative legacy. And Jesus Christ left a positive legacy.

Any time you set out to do some great work, it requires a degree of surrender. To get excellent grades in school you must surrender leisure time. To become physically fit, you must surrender junk food. Excelling to the top of your game, whether it be your career or anything else you set out to do is not easy. You must surrender laziness. And so it is with leaving a Godly legacy.

The Bible gives us true to life examples of people who left exemplary legacies so we could learn from them. Abraham was a man who left an incredible legacy. It began with a promise the he received from God, Himself! God called upon Abraham to go out from his country and relatives to live in an unknown land, and he did! He obeyed God because he believed God. Faith is the key. Abraham believed God's Word, followed it unconditionally, and left a legacy that we can all emulate.

"And He (God) took him outside and said, Now look toward the heavens, and count the stars, if you are able to count them. And He said to him, So shall your descendants be." Genesis 15:5

God promised Abraham that his descendants would be innumerable, too many to count. When we arrive at Gen 22, God wants to see what Abraham is really made of. Actually, He wants Abraham to see what he is made of.

"Now it came about after these things, that God tested Abraham, and said to him, "Abraham!" And he said, "Here I am."

He said, "Take now your son, your only son, whom you love, Isaac, and go to the land of Moriah, and offer him there as a burnt offering on one of the mountains of which I will tell you."

Did you ever say to God, "Enough is enough!" "Haven't I been through enough?" Not Abraham.

The most important thing to him was his legacy. Abraham rose early in the morning, got Isaac up, gathered some firewood and began the trip to Mount Moriah. They arrived at the mountain three days later and Isaac asked a question that must have stung Abraham's heart.

"Isaac spoke to Abraham his father and said, "My father!" And he said, Here I am, my son. And he said, Behold, the fire and the wood, but where is the lamb for the burnt offering?"

That is a harder question than your 5 year old asking, "Where did I come from?"

Abraham replied, "We're going to trust God on this one, son."

Is there a difficult question in your life right now? Is the answer fleeting? Perhaps the true answer is, I'm going to trust God on this one.

"Then they came to the place which God had told him. Abraham built the altar there and arranged the wood, and bound his son Isaac and laid him on the altar, on top of the wood. Abraham stretched out his hand and took the knife to slay his son."

This is a mystifying scene. It shows us how much Isaac trusted his father. Abraham has left his home, family and friends, all that he knew and cherished. Now, he is surrendering all that was vital to his life, his one and only son. This is all a part of making his legacy. If Abraham is going to be the father of the faithful then he needs great faith. And if he is going to be the father of a great race, he needs an heir. Yet, God is calling on him to surrender the heir.

Abraham is thinking, God is going to make me father of a great nation, but now He is taking my son, my heir. This is difficult to figure out. Have you been there? But God doesn't give us all the answers all the time. His will is often like a wind that blows against us. It seems to hinder our progress. Sometimes being in the midst of what God is doing just doesn't make any sense. There are times that He wants us to just trust Him. That's faith.

"Think not, O soul of man, that Abraham's was a unique and solitary experience. It is simply a specimen and pattern of God's dealings with all souls who are prepared to obey Him at whatever cost." F.B. Meyer

"After thou has patiently endured, thou shall receive the promise." Anonymous

What would you say you believe to be vital to you in the pursuit of your own life? I would say that it can all be reduced down to "self." Self is what we adorn, protect, defend, promote, comfort and entertain. And what is self but the Sin Nature! The sin nature is that part of you that gives you a propensity to be independent from God. Independence from God results in rebellion against God. We are told in I Samuel 23 that rebellion against God is as the sin of witchcraft.

Think of how difficult it was and what great faith in God it took for Abraham to surrender his son to God. Your self or sin nature is as dear to you as Abraham's son. But Abraham was willing to surrender and that allowed him to leave us an incredibly, awesome legacy.

"Abraham stretched out his hand and took the

knife to slay his son. But the angel of the LORD called to him from heaven and said, "Abraham, Abraham!" And he said, "Here I am."

Abraham had an audience in heaven. How often do we think about that? Do you think about the audience in heaven watching you at work? How about at home or anywhere else you find yourself? The audience does not consist of people you know or do not know but the audience is the angels of God. They are watching and learning as you live in faith.

"He said, Do not stretch out your hand against the lad, and do nothing to him; for now I know that you fear God, since you have not withheld your son, your only son, from Me."

Abraham's willingness to surrender his son demonstrated he meant business with God. Because Abraham trusted God, he saw the matter right to the end and found a ram caught in the thicket as a substitute sacrifice. You see, God always knows what He is going to do. This resulted in God's commendation to him. Here comes the legacy.

"I will greatly bless you, and I will greatly multiply your seed as the stars of the heavens and as the sand which is on the seashore; and your seed shall possess the gate of their enemies. In your seed all the nations of the earth shall be blessed, because you have obeyed My voice."

If you want to leave a Godly legacy surrender is the pathway. How you will be remembered will be determined by what you surrender. When you surrender things to God, He gives them back for He is only looking for your heart, not what you surrender to Him.

Abraham, the earthly founder of the family of faith must begin by losing himself and his only son, as did the Heavenly Father, the Founder of the family of Christ did for us.

CHAPTER 3
A LEGACY OF WORDS

A reputation is how you are remembered while you are alive. A legacy is how you are remembered after you are gone. The legacy that you are creating begins while you are alive. But how will you be remembered after you are gone?

We will now begin to examine some types of legacies that we can leave behind, as a remembrance to our being here on the earth. One important way we will be remembered is by the words we spoke.

Jesus spoke some harsh words but He is still remembered by His grace in dealing with people. He said to a certain group of people. "You brood of vipers."

Wow! What got Jesus so ticked off? A little earlier, Jesus healed a man with a withered hand and the Pharisees said Jesus' power came from Satan. So Jesus comments;

"How can you, being evil, speak what is good? For the mouth <u>speaks out of that which fills the heart</u>."

That's the key. The heart feeds the mouth. You could say the mouth is the overflow of the heart.

Jesus gives a lesson on words.

"The good man brings out of his good treasure what is good; and the evil man brings out of his evil treasure what is evil." Matthew 12:35

The word "treasure" *thesouros* means a deposit or wealth. It is where we get our word thesaurus, a book that contains a deposit or wealth of words. Therefore, whatever is stored in the heart, will be brought out through the words that you speak. Jesus continues,

"But I tell you that every <u>careless</u> word that people speak, they shall give an accounting for it in the day of judgment." Matthew 12:36

"Carless" means idle, barren, useless and unprofitable.

Ask yourself, What good is something that is useless? What good is something that is unprofitable?

One Greek scholar said;

"It has no legitimate work, no office, no business, but is morally useless and unprofitable." (Vincent)

Jesus brings the verdict.

"For by your words you will be justified, and by your words you will be condemned." Matthew 12:37

Your words will either make you innocent or guilty.

You judge and pronounce sentence upon yourself by the words that you speak. Because this is such a serious issue and it brings judgment upon misuse of the tongue, let's cite some proverbs concerning it.

1. The tongue is very powerful.
"Death and life are in the power of the tongue." Proverbs 18:21
Words can either pick you up or bring you down. Words are probably one of the strongest forces in all the world.

2. It is just as evil to listen to an unprofitable tongue as it is to have one.
"An evildoer listens to wicked lips; a liar pays attention to a destructive tongue." Proverbs 17:4
Here, God is focused, not on the one doing the talking but on the one doing the listening.

After 3 years of researching gossip, Indiana University sociologist Donna Elder has identified an important dynamic involved in gossip. She discovered that the initial negative statement was not the starting point for gossip. The critical turning point was in the response to the gossip.

For example, "She's a real snob," is not the start of gossip. It's when someone "agrees" that the gossip first begins. This leads us to our next proverb.

3. Speak the truth with your tongue. God has given us a beautiful gift, the gift of speech. Just like music, it can be perverted or it can bless. Unlike the animals, we have the ability to communicate our thoughts to one another.
"He who rebukes a man will afterward find more favor than he who flatters with the tongue." Proverbs 28:23

4. Proper use of the tongue protects you from trouble.

"He who guards his mouth and his tongue, guards his soul from troubles." Proverbs 21:23

5. Leave a positive legacy with your tongue.

"A soothing tongue is a tree of life, but perversion in it crushes the spirit." Proverbs 15:4

"The tongue of the righteous is as choice silver, the heart of the wicked is worth little." Proverbs 10:20

The words that we speak are like someone wearing perfume in a room. When the person is gone, the fragrance is still there. The effects of our words are like that.

6. There is a choice between two legacies.

"There is one who speaks rashly like the thrusts of a sword, but the tongue of the wise brings healing." Proverbs 12:18

Wisdom has nothing to do with I.Q. Wisdom is God's wisdom in action. With God's wisdom, I speak of the positive traits of a person and not the negative. I think we can all agree, words are weighty. Someone once said words are like feathers on a doorstep. Once they are laid there, there's no getting them back. Leave a positive legacy by the words that you speak. Did you ever say, I wish I didn't say that?" But they are feathers on a doorstep. You can run as fast as you can but you will never get them back. Even if what you said is forgiven, the scar remains for life.

"Like apples of gold in settings of silver is a word spoken in right circumstances." Proverbs 25:11

This proverb speaks of a beautiful, ornate

decoration in early Eastern culture; very expensive and very decorative for a bed chamber. It was the height of sophistication and elegance.

This is what we as members of the Body of Christ need to focus on. We should be elegant and sophisticated in our words in the way we dress our hearts. Because the mouth speaks from what fills the heart.

So how do I leave a positive legacy of words?

I guard my heart. I fill my heart with God's word. I watch over my heart with all diligence. I remember that my heart is like a well. Only what is in there will come out and I am responsible for what is in there. Do this and you will be remembered for the kindness that you spoke to others.

CHAPTER 4
A LEGACY OF KINDNESS

Who wants to be remembered after they are gone as a stinker? Who wants to be remembered as a cheapskate? Who wants to be remembered as someone who made life all about them? No one! We want to leave a positive legacy. To leave a positive legacy you must do positive things. A positive legacy can leave a happy reminder in the hearts of people. Like a flower in bloom, it leaves a sweet fragrance for others to enjoy. Isn't that a great way a follower of Christ is to be remembered?

In this chapter we have a glimpse into the future regarding those who have left a legacy of kindness. In Matthew 25 we see Jesus in all of His glory.

"But when the Son of Man comes in His glory, and all the angels with Him, then He will sit on His glorious throne. All the nations will be gathered before Him." Matthew 25:31-32

Can you see it? Here is Jesus in all of His glory. The time has come and life on earth is no longer as we know it. Human history has been consummated. It has run its course and reached its goal. People are standing before the glorious Lord, the King of kings and Lord of lords. This is what will happen on that day.

"He will separate them from one another, as the shepherd separates the sheep from the goats;
    and He will put the sheep on His right, and the goats on the left." v.33

This provokes the question, Why the two groups? Which group will I be in?
    We actually all determine which group we will be in while we are alive and living here on the earth. The following verses explain why the separation.

"Then the King will say to those on His right, Come, you who are blessed of My Father, inherit the kingdom prepared for you from the foundation of the world.
    For I was hungry, and you gave Me something to eat; I was thirsty, and you gave Me something to drink; I was a stranger, and you invited Me in; naked, and you clothed Me; I was sick, and you visited Me; I was in prison, and you came to Me." v.34-36

Notice the categories of simple help. We have the giving of food and drink, hospitality, clothing and visitation to the sick and imprisoned. All of these translate into a legacy of kindness.

The rabbis used to say, "As often as a poor man presents himself at thy door, the holy blessed God stands at his right hand. If thou give him alms know that He who stands at his right hand will give thee a reward. But if thou give him not alms, He who stands at his right hand will punish thee."

Ancient travelers would often be destitute of food and drink, sometimes to the point of perishing. Hospitality would be a lifesaver for them.

It wasn't uncommon to find people who were also destitute of proper clothing. Kindness considers the natural needs of people, all people, even strangers. The reward of kindness is also given to those who visit the sick and those in prison.

This is the question of innocence.
"Then the righteous will answer Him, 'Lord, when did we see You hungry, and feed You, or thirsty, and give You something to drink?
And when did we see You a stranger, and invite You in, or naked, and clothe You?
When did we see You sick, or in prison, and come to You?" v.37-39

These people were showing kindness without even realizing the depth of what they were doing. They just did it as a natural result of their spirituality. That is what happens when you have a close relationship with the Lord, Jesus. His nature becomes your nature. Here comes the kicker!

"The King will answer and say to them, Truly I say to you, to the extent that you did it to one of these brothers of Mine, even the least of them, you did it to Me." v.40

God takes personally the kindness that is done to His people. He also takes personally the cruelty that is done to them. In Acts 9, Saul of Tarsus was persecuting the church and Jesus appeared to him and said, "Saul, Saul , why are you persecuting Me?"

This judgment that we will all stand at represents how eternity will reveal what is truly in the hearts of people. Think about the simplicity of leaving a legacy of kindness. A meal, a drink, a welcome or cheering up someone in a hospital or prison are things that anyone do. Though it is help that is uncalculating, it is something the Lord, Himself remembers. Those who showed this kindness were not even aware of the wheightiness of what they were doing. But Jesus took it personally. Those who failed to do so probably thought, O Jesus, if we knew it was You we would have been kind to You. They didn't understand it.

When you see a person in need, picture Jesus. That person may be so close to Him that it might as well be Jesus, Himself.

We will be judged and rewarded according to our reaction to human needs. Knowledge, fame, influence or anything else we have gained in this life will not compare with the kindness God expects us to show to others. Do you want to leave a legacy of kindness?

"For God is not unjust so as to forget your work and the love which you have shown toward His name, in having ministered and in still ministering to the saints." (Hebrews 6:10)

CHAPTER 5
A LEGACY OF FRUIT

When I leave a legacy of words, people remember me by the things that I've said. When I leave a legacy of kindness, people remember me by the things that I've done. When I leave a legacy of fruit, people remember me by what I contributed to life. This is the legacy that makes the world a better place. When people are buried, it is not uncommon to leave an epitaph or a simple statement describing the person's life.

Quotes from tombstones:
"Here lies Lester Moore, took six shots from a .44"

Mel Blanc's epitaph on his headstone in Hollywood Forever Cemetery reads, "That's all folks!"

From a gravestone in Key West, Florida we read,

"At least I know where he's sleeping tonight."

Another one says, "I told you I was sick!"

Will Rogers is known for, "I never met a man I didn't like."

But the one that best describes a legacy of fruit speaks of Christopher Wren of St. Paul's Cathedral in London, England. It reads, "If you seek my monument, look around you."

Leaving a legacy of fruit is about what we leave behind in the lives of people. His legacy was not a fancy, marble statue or building. It was the people around him whom he touched with his life.

A parable;
One day last summer I walked past a beautiful meadow. The grass was as soft and thick and fine as an immense, green Oriental rug. In one corner stood a fine old tree, a sanctuary for numberless birds. The crisp air was sweet and full of their happy songs. Two cows lay in the shade, the very picture of contentment.
Down by the roadside the saucy dandelion mingled his gold with the royal purple of the wild violet. I leaned against the fence for a long time, feasting my hungry eyes and thinking in my soul that God never made a fairer spot than my lovely meadow.
The next day I passed that way again and lo, the hand of the despoiler had been there. A plowman and his great plow, now standing idle in the furrow, had in a day wrought a terrible havoc. Instead of the green grass there was turned up to view the ugly, bare, brown earth. Instead of the singing birds there were only a few hens industriously scratching for worms. Gone were the dandelions and the pretty violets. I said in my grief, How could anyone spoil a thing so fair?

Then my eyes were opened by some unseen hand and I saw a vision, a vision of a field of ripe corn ready for the harvest. I could see the giant, heavily laden stalks in the autumn sun. I could almost hear the music of the wind as it would sweep across the golden tassels. And before I was aware, the brown earth took on a splendor it had not had the day before.

Oh, that we might catch the vision of an abundant harvest when the great Master Plowman comes, as He often does and furrows through our very souls, uprooting and turning under that which we thought most fair, and leaving for our tortured gaze only the bare and the beautiful soul. I know He is no idle husbandman, He purposes a crop. (Samuel Rutherford)

The lesson is this. The beauty and the quiet of the field produce no crops. And so does the idle and sleeping soul. God will dig in His plow and bring disturbances for a while, but then, an abundant harvest will be realized. This is the picture of a fruitful Christianity.

The Old Testament prophet, Isaiah has some wisdom for us regarding the work of the farmer. He writes in Isaiah 28:23-29.

"Give ear and hear my voice. Listen and hear my words. Does the farmer plow continually to plant seed? Does he continually turn and harrow the ground?"

In other words, does he just keep on plowing and never stop plowing? The answer is No. He prepares the ground in order to plant the seed.

"Does he not level its surface and sow dill and scatter cumin and plant wheat in rows, barley in its place and rye within its area?"

Isaiah tells us that God is the ultimate teacher.

The farmer is instructed by God and takes care to use the proper equipment in his work.

"For dill is not threshed with a threshing sledge nor is the cartwheel driven over cummin."

A cartwheel is a large, wheel-like cylinder with sharp teeth pulled by an animal to cut and separate the corn. Isaiah goes on to explain that grain for bread is crushed but not overly crushed. A cartwheel is used to thresh the corn but never to harvest cummin. This would ruin the grain for baking. It takes the right equipment to do the right job. Think of this illustration as God working in your life. One day He may use something light and another day He may use something heavy. Remember, it takes the right equipment to do the right job. And God desires to produce fruit in your life. He ends by noting the origin of wisdom.

"This also comes from the Lord of hosts who has made His counsel wonderful and His wisdom great."

All wisdom comes from God. The History Channel tells us that ancient wisdom came from aliens. I think the aliens are the ones who produce the History Channel. Actually, ancient wisdom comes from God, Creator of all things.

It is apparent that God works in the lives of His people. He is plowing, turning over, planting and cutting. This comes in the way of disturbance. He is upsetting the soil. He turns over the soil of your heart in order to plant the seed of His word there. But all with the intention of reaping. What is reaped from our lives, the harvest, is our legacy of fruit.

Once we realize the farmer's wisdom to produce his crops has come from God, we begin to understand how

God uses that same wisdom to cultivate our hearts for fruitfulness. This leads us to learn about the fruit that He desires to produce within us. Paul's letter to the Galatians outlines this fruit in Galatians 5:22-23.

"But the fruit of the Spirit is love, joy, peace, patience, kindness, goodness, faithfulness, gentleness, self-control; against such things there is no law."

All of these together make up one fruit. When you have all nine parts, you have the fruit. This happens when you yield yourself to God and let the Holy Spirit do His work in your soul, even through the disturbances. Love is the leader of the graces. It is God's unconditional love toward us that we extend toward others. Faith is good but it is only temporary. When we get to heaven, we won't need faith, we can walk by sight. But love will endure forever. The Apostle Paul said in I Corinthians 13 that anything we do apart from love has no meaning with God. Love gives value to what we do.

Joy is another aspect of this fruit. It means to have a calm delight. Imagine yielding yourself to God so much that when He turns over the soil of your heart, you can still allow the Holy Spirit to produce this calm delight within you.

Peace is the mutual peace that you share with others. When God has His way in your life, you remain at peace with people. Sometimes, when we get upset and we take it out on others. This is where we have to stop and realize that God is working in our lives to teach us how to be at peace in adverse circumstances.

Patience is fortitude and long-suffering. It is figuratively the waiting for the crops to grow. After the farmer plants the seed, he knows he has to wait for the seed to grow. There is a process of growth that must take place. While the farmer is waiting for the crops to grow, he is off doing something else, something constructive. He is not sitting watching the seed grow. While we are waiting on the Lord we are doing something constructive with our lives.

Kindness is excellent demeanor. When you are kind it shows. Kindness never remains a secret, it becomes public. We saw this legacy in a previous chapter. Don't you love it when people are kind to you? And you love it even more when you are kind to people! It's a beautiful way to go through life. When you are kind it even makes you better looking. That's because when you are kind, you are joyful, positive and your countenance is glowing. There are so many people around today, who look like they've been baptized in lemon juice – sour puss. No! God wants to turn you into someone that has an excellent demeanor. You walk into a room and the room lights up. Ask yourself, Would people rather see me walk into a room or walk out of a room?

Goodness is the ability to abstain from the appearance of evil and to do good to the body and souls of your fellow man. Goodness is an action. It is not the avoidance of doing bad but the action of doing good.

Faithfulness is trust plus action. Many Christians are faithful in their mind but not faithful in their lives. Your life should complement your faith, your belief system.

Gentleness is mildness, humility. A gentle person is someone who doesn't take things by force. This person is mild enough to wait on God. This is contrary to anger and revenge.

Self-control is temperance, self-government. We struggle with this one. The Apostle James said that if you can control the horse's mouth with a bridle, you can control the whole horse. The same with the rudder of a ship. If we can control the tongue, we can control the whole person.

God is the great Plowman working in the field of our lives, not just to plant His Word but that it would grow. And when we submit to the Holy Spirit in our lives, the fruit begins to grow. Let God plow up your life, plant His Word within you and let the Holy Spirit have His way. Do this every day. When you leave this life perhaps your tombstone will say "Here lies one who bore God's fruit.

CHAPTER 6
A LEGACY OF THANKFULNESS

Have you noticed that these legacies leave a positive reminder in the hearts of people? They are good things that people remember us for. The nice things we said, the kind things we did and the fruit that we bore are all a sweet fragrance to others. You become like a flower in bloom to the people in your life. Each of our lives will either be a sweet fragrance to others or an offensive odor. We make the choice.

A legacy of thankfulness will reflect how you are remembered not only by people, but especially how we are remembered by God. We will use Paul's letter to the Ephesians in chapter 5.

"And do not get drunk with wine, for that is dissipation (wastefulness), but be filled with the Spirit. Speaking to one another in psalms and hymns and spiritual songs, singing and making melody with your heart to the Lord; always giving thanks for all things in the name of our Lord Jesus Christ to God, even the Father."

This is the basis for leaving a legacy of thankfulness. <u>Always giving</u> thanks for <u>all things</u> in the name of our Lord Jesus Christ to God, even the Father.

Just as you appreciate thankfulness from others for the things you have done, our Heavenly Father receives the same delight. Sometimes we have a difficult time giving thanks to God, especially when we don't get what we want. Being thankful does not require payment, it only needs recognition of what our Savior already "has" done. We will look at leaving a legacy of thanks from three different perspectives. We will examine what Jesus did, what God has done for us and what we are to do.

As we look at what Jesus did in Matthew 13, we find a dilemma. A multitude of people had come out to hear Him speak and as the day wore on, they became hungry. Though the disciples wanted to send the people home to get something to eat, Jesus decided to feed them.

"He took the seven loaves and the fish; and giving thanks, He broke them and started giving them to the disciples, and the disciples gave them to the people." Jesus fed a multitude of people that day. Here, He was thankful for what God had given Him, though it was only a little. If you are thankful for the little you have, do you think God would turn it into a lot?

One day an unexpected event occurred. Lazarus, the brother of Mary and Martha had died. He was also a dear friend to Jesus. Jesus was summoned to the tomb to see what He might do. He approached the tomb and prayed to His Father and part of the prayer said;

"Father, I thank You that You have heard Me." God hadn't yet answered Jesus' prayer to raise Lazarus from the dead, but He was thankful just for the privilege of asking. I wonder, how often we are thankful to God, just for listening to us!

Perhaps the most difficult time for Jesus to be thankful was at the Last Supper. The Last Supper was a memorial He was leaving with the disciples. His body was going to be sacrificed and his blood would be shed on the cross of Calvary.

"And when He had taken some <u>bread</u> and given thanks… And when He had taken a <u>cup</u> and given thanks,"

Though He knew He was going to die a horrible death for the sins of mankind, He was thankful. He was thankful He could redeem lost man back to a relationship with Himself.

The second aspect of leaving a legacy of thankfulness is found in what God has done for us.

2 What God has done.

1. God has made us free from the power of sin:

"But thanks be to God that though you were slaves of sin, you became obedient from the heart to that form of teaching to which you were committed, and having been freed from sin, you became slaves of righteousness." Romans 6:17-18

2. He has given us victory over death:

"Thanks be to God, who gives us the victory through our Lord Jesus Christ." I Corinthians 5:17

3. He has given us the gift of Christ, His Son.

"Thanks be to God for His indescribable gift!" II Corinthians 9:15

4. He has given us an inheritance

"Giving thanks to the Father, who has qualified us to share in the inheritance of the saints in Light." Colossians 1:12

Peter said "Our inheritance is; imperishable and undefiled and will not fade away, reserved in heaven for you." I Peter 1:4

3. What we are to do.

1. When you pray, be thankful.

"Be anxious for nothing, but in everything by prayer and supplication with thanksgiving let your requests be made known to God." Philippians 4:6

"Devote yourselves to prayer, keeping alert in it with an attitude of thanksgiving." Colossians 4:2

2. During the course of your day.

"Whatever you do in word or deed, do all in the name of the Lord Jesus, giving thanks through Him to God the Father." Colossians 3:17

It is dangerous not to be thankful. The danger is that you would forget God and become darkened in your understanding.

"For even though they knew God, they did not honor Him as God or give thanks, but they became futile in their speculations, and their foolish heart was darkened." Romans 1:21

Now, who knows more then the inhabitants of

heaven why we should be thankful.

"And all the angels were standing around the throne and around the elders and the four living creatures; and they fell on their faces before the throne and worshiped God, saying, Amen, blessing and glory and wisdom and thanksgiving and honor and power and might, be to our God forever and ever. Amen." Revelation 7:11-12

To leave a legacy of thankfulness, just be thankful. Not only will people remember you this way but so will the Lord.

"Always giving thanks for all things in the name of our Lord Jesus Christ to God, even the Father." Ephesians 5:20

CHAPTER 7
A LEGACY OF MOTHERHOOD

If a legacy is how you are going to be remembered long after you are gone, isn't it fitting to be cognizant of the life you are living in the present?

The role of motherhood was created by God, but over the years, it has taken on a different tone. It's a very important role. A young girl in school was overheard by her teacher as she struggled putting on a pair of bulky rain boots. "Mothers, they're never around when you need them."

Many children love their moms, and they have good intentions, but sometimes it doesn't come out right. A young boy who loved his mom bragged to her; "When I grow up, I'm going to buy you an electric can opener, an electric toaster, an electric stove and an electric chair."

But perhaps the one you feel is true the most is the one where a girl wanted her daddy to tell her a story. He wove together a tale that involved slaves. After he finished his story, she asked; What's a slave daddy? He explained it the best he could. When he was through, the little girl looked up at her daddy and asked, Is that what mommy is?

Yes, Motherhood is quite an institution.

The true role of Motherhood can only be understood through the Scriptures. Let's look at three aspects of motherhood that will help us to understand Motherhood as a Godly legacy.

Let's begin with Mary, the mother of the humanity of Jesus.

1. The Mystery of Motherhood;

Many people are familiar with the Christmas story and the birth of Jesus in the Gospel of Luke, chapter 2. The angel, Gabriel was sent from God to a virgin named Mary, and she was engaged to a man named Joseph. The angel said to her;

"Hail favored one! The Lord is with you. Now this greeting surprised Mary. But she was very perplexed at this statement, and kept pondering what kind of salutation this was."

The angel explained that she had been chosen by God to bring the Savior into the world. And you will call His name, Jesus. Mary questioned how that could happen as she was yet a virgin. Gabriel replied that the Holy Spirit would cause the conception of Jesus.

For us today, Mary represents the moms who are going to be used greatly by God. Mary believed God's messenger, submitted to God's plan, risked what others would think and raised her Son and prepared Him for life.

There is a great mystery here. The mystery is that God entrusts the birth of the Savior with the role of the mom.

I wonder if Mary saw the Word of God unfolding right in her very own life? She was certainly instructed with the teachings of the Old Testament. God said to the serpent after the fall of man

"And I will put enmity between you and the woman, And between your seed and her seed; He shall bruise you on the head, And you shall bruise him on the heel." Genesis 3:15

Did May realize that "she" was the woman and Jesus was the seed? Probably not, as of yet anyway.

Mary would experience the joy of her Son coming in to the world and the sorrow of her Son going out of the world, His birth and death.

The next aspect of Motherhood is the Sorrow of Motherhood.
Jesus was born the way any other boy was born, except that His birthplace was a stable for keeping animals. He grew up a normal childhood, his father being a carpenter and Mary was a stay at home mom.

At twelve years old Jesus began demonstrating a unique hunger and insight into the Old Testament Scriptures. Thirty-three years after His birth Mary finds herself watching the most horrific abuse anyone could experience, and it was happening to her Son. Jesus was finally led to the cross and the Bible tells us;

"And all His acquaintances and the women who accompanied Him from Galilee were standing at a distance, seeing these things." Luke 23:49

They were helpless to prevent it or even to understand what was happening.

John records that Jesus saw His mother standing there while He was hanging on the cross. He spoke to her, but she could only listen. He told her that the disciple, John would take care of her and that she should see him as her son. This was a true experience of aching hearts and flowing tears. And yet, it was prophesied to happen many years before.

"My loved ones and my friends stand aloof from my plague; And my kinsmen stand afar off." Psalm 38:11

Perhaps the saying is true, "There is no greater sorrow than the sorrow of a mother for her child." But that is part of motherhood. Motherhood has a mystery about it. There are times of sorrow in it. Ah, but the joy of motherhood is unspeakable.

3. The Joy of Motherhood

The Apostle Paul gave some wisdom to young Timothy regarding women.

"But women will be preserved through the bearing of children if they continue in faith and love and sanctity with self-restraint." I Timothy 2:15

This means that God will use the woman to bring forth the Savior for the preservation of the human race. Perhaps the most important of all aspects of Motherhood is that it was through Motherhood that God chose to reconcile the world to Himself, by allowing the woman to bring the Savior into the world.

As one writer said;

"However, though Eve was first in the

transgression, and brought death on herself, her husband, and all her posterity, the female sex shall be saved (equally with the male) through child-bearing - through bringing forth the Savior, if they live in faith, and love, and chastity, with that sobriety which I have been recommending."

A Mother's Prayer

I wash the dirt from little feet
And as I wash, I pray
Lord keep them ever pure and true to walk the
narrow way

I wash the dirt from little hands
And earnestly I ask
Lord may they ever yield to the humblest task

I wash the dirt from little knees and pray
Lord, may they be the place where victories are
won and orders sought from Thee.

I scrub the clothes that soil so soon and pray
Lord, may her dress throughout eternal ages be
Thy robe of righteousness.

E'er many hours shall pass,
I know I'll wash these again
And there'll be dirt upon her dress
Before the day shall end.

But as she journeys on through life
And learns of pain and want
Lord, keep her precious little heart cleansed
From all sin and stain

For soap and water cannot reach where Thou alone
can see
Her hands and feet, these I can wash,

But Lord, I trust her heart to Thee.

CHAPTER 8
A LEGACY OF FATHERHOOD

Like Motherhood, Fatherhood brings with it its own challenges and difficulties. The roles of both mother and father both possess their unique challenges. Parents strive to do the best they can to raise their children and most would agree that there is a learning curve to raising them. A father can and should leave behind a legacy of Godly children. And as it is with the moms, a day is set aside to honor those men blessed with the role of father.

Here is what some people said about Father's Day:

A father is a man who accuses the merchants of setting aside this annual day in June so they can get rid of their leftover Christmas ties and shaving lotions – but they love it anyway.

One little boy said; Father's Day is just like Mother's Day, only you don't spend as much on the present.

When we spoke about leaving a legacy of motherhood, we looked at Mary, the mother of the humanity of Jesus. We saw the mystery of motherhood; it's a miracle. We noted the sorrow of motherhood brings heartache. The joy of motherhood was due to the fact that she brought the Savior into the world.

But what about fathers? The Perfect Father, God our Father in heaven, provides some insight for earthly fathers to help them leave a legacy of Godly children.

Fathers on the earth are far from perfect. But our Father in heaven is the model of perfection – He is God; holy, righteous, just and love.

It's interesting to note, God is not called "Father" in the Old Testament. He is referred to as God, Jehovah and other Hebrew names, but not Father.

When Jesus was on the earth He introduced God as Father. When He taught the disciples to pray, He said pray like this; "Our Father, who is in heaven..." This means God has a domain. We know that He is spirit and is everywhere present. But He does have a domain, a place that He calls His own - heaven. So we can draw our example from our Father in heaven.

God is also a forgiving Father. Jesus also said, "For if you forgive others for their transgressions, your heavenly Father will also forgive you." Mt 6:14

This is to show that our heavenly Father wants us to "get along" with each other, by forgiving one another. He is also perfect. But don't lose heart men, we've already said that no earthly father is perfect. "Therefore you are to be perfect, as your heavenly Father is perfect." Mt 5:48

The word "perfect" means complete. He is not lacking in anything. He is self-sufficient and self-dependent. God tells us in His Word;

"For every beast of the forest is Mine, The cattle on a thousand hills. I know every bird of the mountains, And everything that moves in the field is Mine. If I were hungry I would not tell you, For the world is Mine, and all it contains." Psalm 50:10-12

Our heavenly Father is also giving.

"For God so loved the world, that He gave His only begotten Son, that whoever believes in Him shall not perish, but have eternal life. For God did not send the Son into the world to judge the world, but that the world might be saved through Him." John 3:16-17

God gives what the need of the moment calls for. Mankind needed redemption, and God arranged for the price for sin to be paid so we could be reconciled back to Him. Our heavenly Father is very giving.

Let's now make a human comparison and try to understand true fatherhood. A human father also needs a domain. The Scriptures tell us in Proverbs 21:9 "It is better to live in a corner of a roof than in a house shared with a contentious woman."

"Contentious" means one who causes strife, discord or quarreling. The father needs a home where there is a spirit of peace, rest and security. This atmosphere will create a sense of safety for the children.

Proverbs 27:15 tells us why.

"A constant dripping on a day of steady rain and a contentious woman are alike." Who needs a leaky roof?

As God our Father is forgiving, so should the

earthly father be forgiving. Someone once noted:

> "If a child lives with hostility, he learns violence.
> If a child lives with ridicule, he leans to be shy.
> If a child lives with shame, he learns to feel guilty.
> If a child lives with encouragement, he learns confidence.
> If a child lives with praise, he learns to appreciate.
> If a child lives with fairness, he learns justice.
> If a child lives with approval, he learns to like himself.
> If a child lives with acceptance and friendship, he learns to love others.
> If a child receives forgiveness, he learns to give forgiveness."

As God is complete, so should the earthly father be complete. Completeness comes from wisdom. Let's note where wisdom comes from.

"The fear of the Lord is the beginning of wisdom." Pr 1:7

"His delight is in the word of the Lord." Psalm2

"He saves his life by losing it." Matthew 5

Finally, as God our Father is giving, so should the earthly father be giving. Our heavenly Father gave us the greatest gift, the gift of His Son. John3:16-17

In the giving of His Son, He gave Himself.

The best thing the earthly father can give is himself, as an example to his children. Perhaps this poem will illustrate.

There are little eyes upon you, and they are watching night and day

There are little ears that quickly take in every word you say

There are little hands all eager to do everything you do

And a little boy who's dreaming of the day he'll be

like you.

You're the little fellow's idol, you're the wisest of the wise

In his little mind, about you no suspicions ever rise.

He believes in you devoutly, holds that all you say and do

He will say and do in your way, when he's grown up just like you

There's a wide-eyed little fellow, who believes you're always right

His ears are always open and he watches day and night

You are setting an example everyday in all you do

For the little boy who's waiting to grow up to be like you.

No human father is perfect, but if we learn to emulate our heavenly Father, we can leave a Godly legacy to our children who follow after us.

CHAPTER 9
A LEGACY OF GODLY CHILDREN

We understand that our legacy is made up of our words, deeds and attitudes. People will remember us through these things. But there is another, very vital legacy many people will leave behind, their children.

If you remember the Art Linkletter show, he had a segment where "children said the darndest things." I would like to share with you a few letters that some children wrote to their pastors.

Dear Pastor Letters:

Dear Pastor, I know God loves everybody but He never met my sister. Yours sincerely, Arnold. Age 8,

Dear Pastor, Please say in your sermon that Peter Peterson has been a good boy all week. I am Peter Peterson. Sincerely, Pete. Age 9,

Dear Pastor, My father should be a minister. Every day he gives us a sermon about something. Robert, Age 11,

Dear Pastor, I'm sorry I can't leave more money in

the plate, but my father didn't give me a raise in my allowance. Could you have a sermon about a raise in my allowance? Love, Patty. Age 10,

Dear Pastor, My mother is very religious. She goes to play bingo at church every week even if she has a cold. Yours truly, Annette. Age 9,

Dear Pastor, I would like to go to heaven someday because I know my brother won't be there. Stephen. Age 8,

Dear Pastor, I think a lot more people would come to your church if you moved it to Disneyland. Loreen. Age 9,

Dear Pastor, I hope to go to heaven some day but later than sooner. Love, Ellen, age 9.

Dear Pastor, Please say a prayer for our Little League team. We need God's help, or a new pitcher. Thank you. Alexander. Age 10,

Dear Pastor, My father says I should learn the Ten Commandments. But I don't think I want to because we have enough rules already in my house. Joshua. Age 10,

Dear Pastor, I liked your sermon on Sunday. Especially when it was finished. Ralph, Age 11,

Perhaps the one that speaks to us the most is a greeting card a young boy gave to his dad. The cover of a Sandy Boynton greeting card: "I'm so glad you're my dad, and I think you're happy I'm your kid." Inside it reads, "Mostly."

Let's learn about the importance of leaving a legacy of Godly children:

1. They are a gift from God:

We begin by understanding where children came from and why we have them.

"Behold, children are a gift of the LORD." Psalm 127:3

A "gift" is something inherited, an heirloom. Something inherited did not originally belong to you. You received it from someone else. Here, children are received from God.

2. Leave them something of value:

"A good man leaves an inheritance to his children's children." Proverbs 13:22

Here it is speaking about money or something material. The story of the Prodigal Son is fitting here. The father divided his estate between his two sons. The father was able to do this because he worked hard and built up his farm so he could leave his sons an inheritance. Spiritually speaking, Jesus shares His inheritance with us;

"Giving thanks to the Father, who has qualified us to share in the inheritance of the saints in Light." Colossians 1:12

But here, I'd like to make the application of leaving a spiritual inheritance. It is important to leave your children a moral, spiritual and ethical legacy. They need role models from which to draw instruction for their own lives.

"A good man leaves an inheritance to his children's children."

If the grandchildren have an inheritance, it stands to reason that the children do as well. Let's look at this inheritance as being three-fold:

- Prayer: the good man offers up prayers to God for his children.
- Advice: the good man imparts Godly wisdom to His children. He warns them of dangers and encourages them to do good.

"The fear of the LORD is the beginning of knowledge; fools despise wisdom and instruction. Hear, my son, your father's instruction And do not forsake your mother's teaching." Proverbs 1:7-8

Parents not only leave a legacy of prayers to God and Godly advice but also a good example. Parents, may use words to teach your children, but actions speak louder than words.

Children learn by imitating. Because they love their parents, they seek to emulate them. So parents must be aware of what they model before their children. Such behaviors as swearing, smoking, drinking, and gambling would not be considered a healthy legacy.

Why do children swear at their mothers? Because their fathers taught them how. Why does the sin of alcoholism go from generation to generation? Because their parents taught them. Can you see the importance of leaving a Godly legacy?

This leads us to the third aspect of leaving a Godly legacy to our children:

3. The fear of the Lord:

"In the fear of the LORD there is strong confidence, and his children will have refuge." Proverbs 14:26

You leave a safe haven when you instruct them in the fear and respect of God. Like a port in a storm, they can find refuge in their relationship with God.

"Train up a child in the way he should go, even when he is old he will not depart from it." Proverbs 22:6

To "train" means to dedicate. Literally, initiate the child at the opening (the mouth) of his path. The phrase "way he should go" means the road he should travel. This is instruction for Godly living.

Though a parable, it is not a guarantee. It is a principle to live by. But, it does "help" to insure the child to make the right decisions when he or she has reached maturity. There is one danger parents should be aware of and that is failure to leave a Godly legacy for their children.

"The rod and reproof give wisdom, but a child who gets his own way brings shame to his mother." Proverbs 29:15

Reason being, "Foolishness is bound up in the heart of a child." Pr 22:15

These are the steps to leaving a Godly legacy for your children. Realize that as a parent you have been entrusted by God with His children. Provide for them the best you can so they can have an inheritance. Instruct them in the fear of the Lord. Work at training them up. And let them know you're happy they are your kids.

CHAPTER 10
A LEGACY OF COURAGE

Boldness is an important part of life. It gives us the confidence to keep moving forward, even in the face of uncertainty, threat and doubt. Without boldness or confidence, nothing great would ever be accomplished.

We will see that for the disciples, "courage was not the absence of fear, but the willingness to push on in the face of it."

As God's people, especially following the resurrection of Christ, we have all the reason to be BOLD in our walk and in our witness.

Let's take a walk back through history to the First Century. Luke is writing to a man named Theopholis concerning the things of Jesus Christ. His manuscript is called "The Acts of the Apostles."

Acts 1

Luke recalls that Jesus appeared to the disciples after the resurrection. He told them to remain in Jerusalem and await the Holy Spirit. He then ascended into heaven, right before their eyes! WOW!

Acts 2

The Day of Pentecost has now arrived – 50 days after Passover (when Jesus was Crucified)

The disciples were all together in a room, praying;

"And suddenly there came from heaven a noise like a violent rushing wind, and it filled the whole house where they were sitting."

They were filled with the Holy Spirit and began speaking with other tongues. They went into the city and proclaimed the Gospel to the various people in Jerusalem in their own foreign languages. The people thought the apostles had been drinking, speaking the way they were but they said it was too early in the morning for that!

In order to leave a legacy of courage, one must possess courage. You find courage when you believe in the resurrected Christ and you are filled with the Holy Spirit. Faith in Christ brings the Holy Spirit and the Holy Spirit brings boldness.

The Apostle Peter was hiding in an upper chamber for fear of the religious crowd who crucified Jesus. But when the Holy Spirit came upon him, great boldness did as well. Peter proclaimed that what was happening was prophesied to happen in the Old Testament.

"And with many other words he solemnly testified and kept on exhorting them, saying, "Be saved from this perverse generation! So then, those who had received his word were baptized; and that day there were added about three thousand souls."

To be "baptized" was a sign that they had come out from Judaism and were now followers of Jesus Christ.

Peter's boldness continued. A little later, Peter and John healed a man who was lame and they also preached Christ had risen from the dead. The same people who crucified Jesus now arrested Peter and John.

As told in Acts 4, "Then Peter, filled with the Holy Spirit, said to them, Rulers and elders of the people, if we are on trial today for a benefit done to a sick man, as to how this man has been made well, let it be known to all of you and to all the people of Israel, that by the name of Jesus Christ the Nazarene, whom you crucified, whom God raised from the dead--by this name this man stands here before you in good health."

"He (Christ) is the stone which was rejected by you, the builders, but which became the chief cornerstone. And there is salvation in no one else; for there is no other name under heaven that has been given among men by which we must be saved."

V.13 speaks of "A Legacy of Courage."

"Now as they observed the confidence of Peter and John and understood that they were uneducated and untrained men, they were amazed, and began to recognize them as having been with Jesus."

It was not their education or intelligence that gave them courage. It was their relationship with Christ!

"He who is taught in spiritual matters by Christ Jesus has a better gift than the tongue of the learned. He who is taught in the school of Christ will ever speak to the point, and intelligibly too; though his words may not have that polish with which they who prefer sound to sense are often carried away." (Adam Clarke)

The religious leaders commanded Peter and John to speak no longer about this Jesus. This was actually the first persecution of the early church after the resurrection.

Peter, in his boldness said, "We cannot stop speaking about what we have seen and heard."

When they were released from jail, they joined the disciples for a time of prayer.

"And when they had prayed, the place where they had gathered together was shaken, and they were all filled with the Holy Spirit and began to speak the word of God with <u>boldness</u>."

Paul the Apostle shared this boldness in Christ when he said, "I am under compulsion; for woe is me if I do not preach the gospel." I Corinthians 9:16

"And with great power the apostles were giving testimony to the resurrection of the Lord Jesus, and abundant grace was upon them all."

How do I want to be remembered, as someone who talked with boldness and confidence about what they believed in or someone who shrunk back from what they believed?

Toward the end of his life, Paul said; "I did not shrink from declaring to you anything that was profitable, and teaching you publicly and from house to house." Acts 20:20

The writer of the book of Hebrews said; "But we are not of those who shrink back to destruction, but of those who have faith to the preserving of the soul." Hebrews 10:9

When we leave a legacy of courage we are not cowards, but courageous. We are believers who act on what they believe.

Why do I need to leave a legacy of courage? He who loses wealth, loses much; he who loses a friend, loses more; but he who loses his courage loses all.

CHAPTER 11
A LEGACY OF GENEROSITY

Giving is one of the greatest joys in life, and yet it is one of the most challenging. It is a means of great blessing; the Apostle Paul said;

> "In everything I showed you that by working hard in this manner you must help the weak and remember the words of the Lord Jesus, that He Himself said, It is more blessed to give than to receive." Acts 20:35

Yet, generosity is a challenge because it puts your faith on trial. You may feel that generous giving threatens your financial security. But Biblical giving doesn't threaten your financial security. Rather, It deepens your trust in God.

Try to remember this thought as we go through this chapter thinking about how we're going to be remembered after we are gone.

"We make a living by what we get,

We make a life by what we give."

Mark chapter 12 gives us this account.

"And He (Jesus), sat down opposite the treasury, and began observing how the people were putting money into the treasury; and many rich people were putting in large sums. A poor widow came and put in two small copper coins, which amount to a cent. Calling His disciples to Him, He said to them, Truly I say to you, this poor widow put in more than all the contributors to the treasury; for they all put in out of their surplus, but she, out of her poverty, put in all she owned, all she had to live on."

Generosity is more of an attitude than it is an action. An act is what we do; an attitude is what we think. Giving doesn't begin with the hand, it begins with the mind. When we think about giving to the work of God, the motivation is two-fold. We are thankful for what He has done for us and we believe that supporting His church and preaching the Gospel saves souls.

The late Peter Marshall, chaplain of the Senate and Presbyterian pastor in Washington, prayed a prayer. The first part of this prayer substantiates true motivational giving. He prayed, "Lord, help me to regulate my giving according to my income, lest Thou should regulate my income according to my giving!"

Let's go back to Jesus' Classroom in Mark chapter 12.

"And He sat down opposite the treasury,"

Jesus just finished warning people about the

ways of the Pharisees. They like to look spiritual in long robes and they relish public attention. They enjoy important seats and places among people. They pray too long and take advantage of widows. Therefore, they are condemned by God.

Jesus sat down, "and began observing how the people were putting money into the treasury; and many rich people were putting in large sums." He was too tired to walk but not too tired to watch. He became an observer of people's giving.

How much do you consider that heaven watches your life? Here, Jesus was watching how much the people were putting in. "Money" speaks of metal money, brass money; coins. Why coins? Because coins make a lot of noise.

"Large sums" meant many coins.

"A poor widow came and put in two small copper coins." Note the contrast; two small copper coins, compared to brass coins the others were putting in. She could only put in copper coins; (remember that). She put in the equivalent of one penny. The lesson begins:

"Calling His disciples to Him,"

Boy, Jesus had it tough! Do you know why Jesus "called His disciples"? Remember earlier, right before this lesson on true giving; Jesus had warned people about the evil of the Pharisees, how they like to look spiritual, take important seats and take advantage of widows. At that time the disciples slinked away. They feared what would happen if people heard Jesus talking this way.

Did you ever hang out with an outspoken person? When they said things that made you cringe, what did you want to do? Probably, get out of there. Jesus often said things that would get a guy killed; things like He was God, like He could forgive sins. Jesus called His disciples back to Him and said;

"Truly I say to you, this poor widow put in more than all the contributors to the treasury; for they all put in out of their surplus, but she, out of her poverty, put in all she owned, all she had to live on."

"All she had to live on" was her livelihood.

Here we are, 2,000 years later, reading about her and learning from her what true giving is. She left a legacy of generosity for following generations.

There is joy in receiving, and greater joy in giving; but only to the mature. A child doesn't understand the joy of giving. He only knows the joy of getting. But once grown, he learns the joy of giving. That says a lot about where you may be spiritually.

Do you see a legacy of giving as a threat to your financial security or as a building of your faith in God?

There is an old story about a very wealthy man who died and went to heaven. An angel guided him on a tour of the celestial city. He came to a magnificent home. "Who lives there?" asked the wealthy man. "Oh," the angel answered, "on earth he was your gardener."

The rich man got excited. If this was the way gardeners live, just think of the kind of mansion in which he would spend eternity. They came to an even more magnificent abode. "Who's is this?" asked the rich man almost overwhelmed.

The angel answered, "She spent her life helping the poor." The rich man was really getting excited now. Finally they came to a tiny eight-by-eight shack with no window and only a piece of cloth for a door. It was the most pitiful home the rich man had ever seen.

"This is your home," said the angel. The wealthy man was flabbergasted. "I don't understand. The other homes were so beautiful. Why is my home so tiny?"

The angel smiled sadly, "I'm sorry," he said. "We did all we could with what you sent us to work with."

Jesus said to a young man who wanted to have eternal life, "If you wish to be complete, go and sell your possessions and give to the poor, and you will have treasure in heaven; and come, follow Me." Matthew 19:21

Another time Jesus spoke about how to leave a legacy of generosity;

"Do not store up for yourselves treasures on earth, where moth and rust destroy, and where thieves break in and steal. *But store up for yourselves treasures in heaven.* Matthew 6:19-20

You can do this when you leave a Legacy of Generosity.

CHAPTER 12
A LEGACY OF SERVICE

A servant is one in the employment of another with out any freedoms at all. Contrary to natural thinking, servanthood is the noblest of professions or social status.

To serve comes from the French word, *server;* from the Latin, *servous.* It means to be a slave, serf.

Serf – a person in feudal servitude bound to his master's land, who is also transferred with the land to a new owner.

Servanthood is an interesting thing. The disciples asked Jesus "Who is the greatest in the kingdom of heaven?" He answered, "The greatest among you shall be your servant." Let's look at the scene in Luke 22.

"And there arose also a dispute among them as to which one of them was regarded to be greatest." Jesus answered with a story:

"And He said to them, The kings of the Gentiles lord it over them; and those who have authority over them are called 'Benefactors." He then introduces the economy of heaven. "But it is not this way with you."

ie. You are different!

"But the one who is the greatest among you must become like the youngest, and the leader like the servant. For who is greater, the one who reclines at the table or the one who serves? Is it not the one who reclines at the table? But I am among you as the one who serves." Leaving a legacy of service is one of the noblest of all legacies.

Mark 10 affords us the best record of the legacy of service that Jesus left us with a little different twist.

"Calling them to Himself, Jesus said to them, You know that those who are recognized as rulers of the Gentiles lord it over them; and their great men exercise authority over them. But it is not this way among you, but whoever wishes to become great among you shall be your servant; and whoever wishes to be first among you shall be slave of all."

Then He brings it home! (Here is the twist)

"For <u>even</u> the Son of Man did not come to be served, but to serve, and to give His life a ransom for many."

Therefore, what Jesus said and did, demonstrated His service to His Father. He said, "I speak just as the Father has told Me." John 12:50

Another time He said, "The works which the Father has given Me to accomplish--the very works that I do-- testify about Me, that the Father has sent Me." John 5:36

Notice the degree to which He served. He served His Father by the things He said and did and to give His life a ransom for many.

Let's talk about followers of Christ. The Apostle Paul encouraged the Christians in Philippi.

"For our citizenship is in heaven, from which also we eagerly wait for a Savior, the Lord Jesus Christ." Philippians 3:20

The word "citizenship" *politeuma,* is where we get the word politics. Citizenship is community, rights and privileges. This phrase was based on Roman citizenship. A citizen of Rome had special rights. He could vote, hold office, and own property. He had legal rights and was immune from some taxes. He also could not be tortured, whipped or crucified. Paul is saying that we are citizens of heaven, therefore, pilgrims on this earth.

A servant is one in the employment of another without any freedoms at all. Living in God's kingdom and purpose is contrary to living in the kingdom and purpose of the world. And as was said, servanthood is the noblest of statuses because it is the role Jesus assumed. You can tell whether you have the heart of a servant by how you act when people treat you like one.

This is what it looks like to be a servant of God.

- It's not how many people serve you but how many people you serve.
- When people come to you they feel better and happier when they leave.

- It's having eyes to see the lostness in a person when you look at them.
- Serve their spiritual needs and do what you can to bring them to Christ, forgiveness and eternal life.

Final illustration:

A rabbi dreamed he had been given the opportunity to see both heaven and hell. He was directed to a closed door and informed that hell existed beyond the doorway.

As he entered the room he was surprised to see a banquet hall that was set for a feast. Everything was exquisitely prepared but all of the diners wailed and moaned in agony, and they were all so skinny.

In the center of the table was a mouthwatering dish of food and each and every person had a very long spoon strapped to their hand. The spoon was long enough for one to reach the food but too long to put it in their mouth. Consequently, they were unable to eat and were shrieking with hunger pains. The horror was more than the Rabbi could bear so he asked to leave.

When he opened the other door, that led to heaven, he was petrified to see the same scene. The same luxurious banquet was set before them. But this time joy replaced the pitiful cries. The difference in the two places was that those in heaven did not cry over their inability to feed themselves. They simply celebrated the privilege of feeding each other with the same long spoons.

Here is what we learn from this story. Live to serve yourself, and you go hungry. Live to serve others and you are fulfilled. When you leave a legacy of servanthood, you leave a picture of a true servant of Jesus Christ; a reminder that you are a pilgrim on this earth, a citizen of heaven; and you travelled a road to real fullness.

CHAPTER 13
A LEGACY OF FAITH

In the eyes of God, a legacy of faith is a precious legacy. In this chapter we will see that people who went before us left their own legacy and their names were written down in the Bible. We will also learn about three aspects of faith; what faith is, what it does and what it gives.

The book of Hebrews is not only a book about faith, it is a book about the faithful, especially chapter 11.

"Now faith is the assurance of things hoped for, the conviction of things not seen." Hebrews 11:1

The word "assurance" means the foundation upon which something stands. The "things hoped for" are that which stand on faith.

"For by it the men of old gained approval."

"Approval" means they bore testimony, were

witnesses. Faith is active and we can actually see it alive and moving in the lives of people. Here is what faith does:

v.4 Faith sacrifices to God.

"By faith Abel offered to God a better sacrifice than Cain, through which he obtained the testimony that he was righteous."

v.5 Faith walks with God.

"By faith Enoch was taken up so that he would not see death; and he was not found because God took him up, for he obtained the witness that before his being taken up he was pleasing to God."

v.7 Faith obeys God, when it doesn't make sense.

"By faith Noah, being warned by God about things not yet seen, in reverence prepared an ark for the salvation of his household."

v.8 Faith follows God's leading, not knowing where He is leading.

"By faith Abraham, when he was called, obeyed by going out to a place which he was to receive for an inheritance; and he went out, not knowing where he was going."

v.9 Faith doesn't get comfortable in this world.

"By faith he (Abraham) lived as an alien in the land of promise, as in a foreign land, dwelling in tents with Isaac and Jacob."

v.11 Faith believes God's promises.

"By faith even Sarah herself received ability to

conceive, even beyond the proper time of life, since she considered Him faithful who had promised."

v.13-15 Faith makes eternity more real than time.

"All these died in faith, without receiving the promises, but having seen them and having welcomed them from a distance, and having confessed that they were strangers and exiles on the earth.
For those who say such things make it clear that they are seeking a country of their own.
And indeed if they had been thinking of that country from which they went out, they would have had opportunity to return."

v.17 Faith makes the ultimate sacrifice .

"By faith Abraham, when he was tested, offered up Isaac, and he who had received the promises was offering up his only begotten son."

v.21 Faith blesses in death.

"By faith Jacob, as he was dying, blessed each of the sons of Joseph, and worshiped."

v.23 Faith honors God's law over man's law.

"By faith Moses, when he was born, was hidden for three months by his parents, because they saw he was a beautiful child; and they were not afraid of the king's edict."

v.24-25 Faith refuses the sinful pleasures of this world.

"By faith Moses, when he had grown up, refused to be called the son of Pharaoh's daughter,

choosing rather to endure ill-treatment with the people of God than to enjoy the passing pleasures of sin."

v.28 Faith believes God's promise of deliverance .

"By faith he (Moses) kept the Passover and the sprinkling of the blood, so that he who destroyed the firstborn would not touch them."

v.29 Faith attempts the impossible.

"By faith they passed through the Red Sea as though they were passing through dry land; and the Egyptians, when they attempted it, were drowned."

v.30 Faith fights unconventional warfare.

"By faith the walls of Jericho fell down after they had been encircled for seven days."

v.31 Faith protects God's people.

"By faith Rahab the harlot did not perish along with those who were disobedient, after she had welcomed the spies in peace."

3. The reward of faith:

v.39-40 The people who lived in faith were approved by God.

"And all these, having gained approval through their faith, did not receive what was promised, because God had provided something better for us, so that apart from us they would not be made perfect."

As you can see, faith is honorable. It accepts the challenges of life but possesses great confidence in God.

Pauley's Legacy
March 31,1984-April 8, 2013

Most people would agree, "To know him was to love him." Pauley was a man who made his dad, Paul Sr. and mom, Debbie very proud. Though a golf enthusiast, the highlight of his life was doing mission work in the Appalachian Mountains of West Virginia.

What people said about Pauley.

"He was a man with a humble spirit."

"People flocked to see him as they did Jesus."

"He was all things to all people."

"Pauley loved to have fun."

The legacy of Pauley Andrade will live on in the hearts of all who were fortunate enough to know him. He is remembered by a heart-shaped flower bed growing to this day at the Mountain Marketplace Mission in Webster County, West Virginia. The flower bed is a fine symbol of Pauley's life because he planted seeds of love wherever he went.

The life of Paul Andrade Jr. was a life well spent. The world is a better place because of him and many people have learned what true Godly love is through Him. He will more than be remembered. He lives on in our hearts.

ABOUT THE AUTHOR

David P. Therrien

Graduated from Gordon Conwell Seminary in Boston, MA with a Masters of Arts Degree In Urban Ministry. He enjoys the four seasons of New England with his wife, Donna and has three sons, Michael, David Jr. and Alex.

Dave writes on matters of faith and encouragement and pastors the wonderful people of New Hope Christian Church in Swansea, MA.

www.newhopecc.tv

Other Resources

You can find other books by
David P. Therrien
at
www.inspiringbooks.org

Email
Inspiringbooksofhope@gmail.com

For CDs and DVDs go to
www.newhopecc.tv

POCKETBOOK SERIES
So far...

Look Up And Be Forgiven Vol. 1
Going Forward In Faith Vol. 2
How To Escape From Guilt & Shame Vol. 3
The Loving Father & The Lost Son Vol. 4
The Story of Mephibosheth Vol. 5
The Brightest Future Ever Vol. 6

ALSO
Beauty In Darkness
Finding HOPE In Distressing Times
GOT Life?
How To Know If You're Really Living
Angel Conversations
Sailing Through Storms
Recovering Lost Ground
A 12 Step Guide to Overcoming Compulsive Behaviors

MEDIA
Check out Dave's radio show
WARV 1590 am dial
Or
Stream it at
WARV.net
Weekdays at 12:30 pm E.T. and
Saturdays at 3 pm.

DVDs & CDs can also be found at
www.newhopecc.tv
MEDIA button

Life is a journey.
Don't look back,
and keep moving!

Made in the USA
Charleston, SC
11 March 2014